GEOGRAPHY FILES

Mountains

Gianna Williams

WAYLAND

GEOGRAPHY FILES

First published in 2007
by Wayland
This book is based on *Geography Fact Files: Mountains* by Anna Claybourne, originally published by Wayland.

Copyright © Wayland 2007

Wayland
338 Euston Road
London NW1 3BH

Wayland Australia
Hachette Children's Books
Level 17/207 Kent Street
Sydney, NSW 2000

Produced by Discovery Books

Subject consultant: Keith Lye

Illustrations: Michael Posen

British Library Cataloguing Publication Data
Williams, Gianna

Mountains. - (Geography files)
1. Mountains - Juvenile literature
I. Title
551.4'32

ISBN-13: 978 07502 5269 0

Printed in China.

Wayland is a division of Hachette Children's Books

Acknowledgements
We are grateful to the following for permission to reproduce photographs: Alamy 19 bottom, 47; Corbis 1 (Galen Rowell), 6 (Bettmann), 9 top (Danny Lehman), 15, 17 (Galen Rowell), 27 (James A Sugar), 28 (Gunther Marx Photography), 39 bottom (Marc Muench), 40 (Dewitt Jones); Corbis Digital Stock 3 bottom inset, 33; FLPA 14 (Steve McCutcheon), 45 (David Hosking); Getty Images front cover (William Smithey Jr); James Davis Travel Photography 5 top, 11 top, 32, 46; Mountain Camera 19 top; Nature Picture Library back cover left (Konstantin Mikhailov), 22 (Konstantin Mikhailov), 25 top (Juan Manuel Borrero); NHPA 29 (T Kitchin and V Hurst); PA Photos 26 (Alison Hargreaves), 31 top (EPA); Rex Features 9 bottom (SIPA), 36 (B Veysett/SIPA), 41 (Lehtikuva Oy), 43 top (SIPA); Robert Harding Picture Library 3 middle inset (Tony Demin/International Stock), 4 (S Sassoon), 12 (Tony Waltham), 20 (Ron Sanford/International Stock), 25 bottom (Tony Waltham), 37 (E Simaner), 39 top (Tony Demin/International Stock); Still Pictures 3 top inset (Peter Weimann), 5 bottom (Roland Seitre), 11 bottom (Alain Compost), 21 top (Peter Weimann), 21 bottom (Fritz Polking), 30 (Hartmut Schwarzbach), 31 bottom (Edward Parker), 34 (John Isaac), 35 top (Adrian Arbib), 35 bottom (Mark Edwards), 38 (Chiaus Lotcher), 42 (Daniel Dancer), 43 bottom (Fritz Polking); Swift Imagery 10 (David Young), 13 (G R Park), 44.

Contents

The words that are explained in the glossary
are printed in **bold**.

What is a mountain?

Everyone knows what a mountain looks like – but what is a mountain? A mountain is a mound of land, with sloping sides, that rises above the land around it.

Mountain ranges

Most mountains are found in mountain ranges. These are long chains or groups of mountains that can stretch for thousands of kilometres. The Andes mountain range reaches all the way down the western side of South America.

▼ The 5,895 m-high Kilimanjaro, in Tanzania, East Africa, seemed magical to many people, because it had snow on top, even though it is in a hot country.

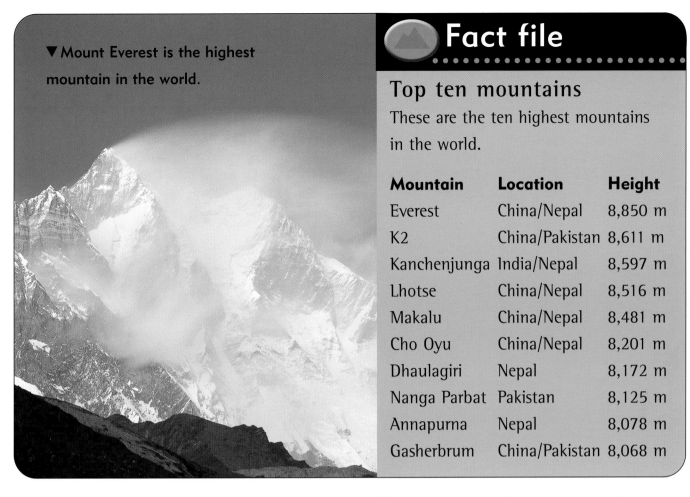

▼ Mount Everest is the highest mountain in the world.

A different world

Mountains are colder and windier than the low lands around them, and there is less air to breathe. Because the conditions on a mountain are different, the wildlife is different too. Mountain animals often have extra-thick fur for keeping warm, or extra-large feet so they don't sink in the snow.

Living in the mountains

Because they are tough places, most mountain areas have been left alone by people. But people do live in mountains, often in small villages. They herd animals, grow crops or work as guides.

▼ A woman, up in the mountains of Bhutan, weaves yak wool.

Where are mountains?

There are mountains all over the world. Mountain regions cover 20 per cent of the land on Earth. There are also mountains under the sea.

The biggest mountains

The highest mountains in the world are in the Himalayas. The Himalayas are in Asia, and lie between the countries of India, China, Pakistan, Nepal and Bhutan. Other big mountain ranges include the Andes, the Alps, the Rockies, the Urals and the Atlas Mountains.

People file

Hannibal

Hannibal was a general from Carthage, in North Africa. Carthage was at war with the Roman Empire. In 218 BC, Hannibal planned an attack on Rome from Spain. He chose to cross the Alps – with elephants – hoping to surprise the Romans. It took his army 15 days to cross the Alps, and many elephants died.

◀ A painting of Hannibal and his army crossing the Alps.

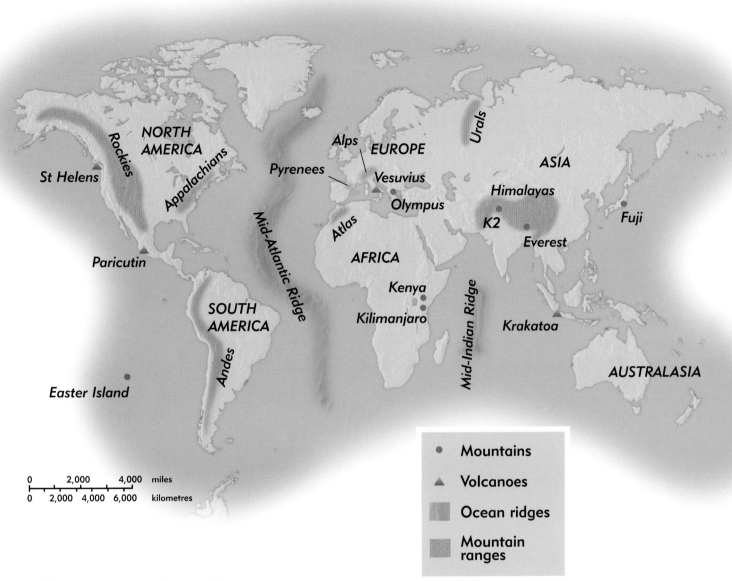

NORTH
AMERICA

Rockies

St Helens

Appalachians

Paricutin

SOUTH
AMERICA

Andes

Easter Island

Mid-Atlantic Ridge

Alps
EUROPE
Pyrenees
Vesuvius
Olympus

Atlas

AFRICA

Kenya

Kilimanjaro

Mid-Indian Ridge

Urals

ASIA

Himalayas

K2

Everest

Krakatoa

Fuji

AUSTRALASIA

| 0 | 2,000 | 4,000 | miles |
| 0 | 2,000 4,000 6,000 | | kilometres |

- • Mountains
- ▲ Volcanoes
- Ocean ridges
- Mountain ranges

▲ This map shows the world's main
mountain ranges and some important
mountain peaks.

Mountains under the sea

There are also mountains under the sea.
One of the biggest undersea mountain
ranges is the Mid-Atlantic Ridge, which
runs down the middle of the Atlantic
Ocean. Sometimes, the peaks of
undersea mountains stick out and form
islands. The island of Iceland is a part of
the Mid-Atlantic Ridge.

Location file

Easter Island

Easter Island is a tiny island in the
Pacific Ocean. Although the island is
small, it's just the tip of a giant
volcano that rises nearly 3,000 m
from the sea floor. People settled on
the island around 1,500 years ago.

Making mountains

Mountains are made when part of the hard, rocky crust that covers the Earth moves upwards. Mountains are named after the way they were made.

Fold mountains

The continents are part of the Earth's crust. The crust is made of huge sections of rock that fit together like a jigsaw. These sections float on the **magma**, a hot liquid rock, inside the Earth. When the sections press against each other, their edges are slowly pushed up into large folds and wrinkles. Most of the Earth's mountain ranges were made this way.

Fault-block mountains

Fault-block mountains are made when a huge block of rock separates from the rest of the crust around it, and it is pushed up or sinks down.

Bulging domes

Dome mountains are a type of mountain made when magma pushes the rock above it upwards.

Fold mountains form when two sections of land push together.

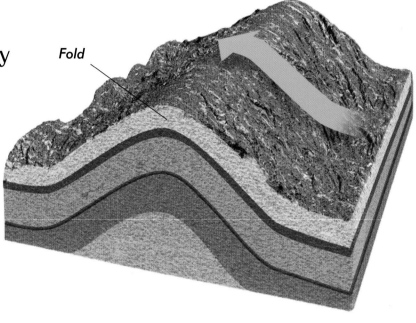

Fold

Fault-block mountains form when a section of land separates from the land around it, and rises or sinks.

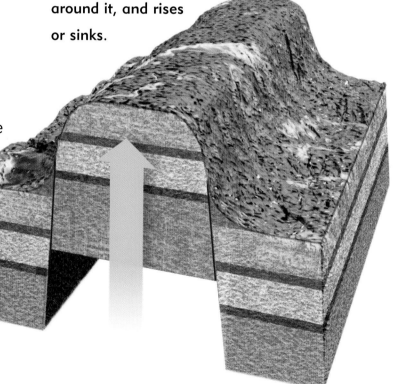

8

Volcanoes

Fold mountains and fault-block mountains take millions of years to form, but a volcano can grow quickly – sometimes in just a few weeks. Volcanoes happen when magma from inside the Earth bursts out, then cools and hardens into rock. Volcanoes are common where sections of the Earth's crust meet, such as in the Andes. Volcanoes can also form in areas where the Earth's crust is thin and magma can push through.

Birth of a volcano

In Mexico in 1943, a farmer named Dominic Pulido noticed a strange crack in his cornfield. Hot ash and lava soon started to pour out of it. After two months, the new volcano, named Paricutin, was over 300 m high. Paricutin has now stopped erupting and is 424 m high.

The folded Himalayas

The Himalayas (below) are fold mountains. They first started to grow 50 million years ago, when the section of rock, called a plate, carrying India pushed against the rest of Asia.

How mountains change

They might look solid, but mountains are changing all the time. Even when mountains are still growing, their peaks wear down over time.

Pushing up

The sections of rock in the Earth's crust move very slowly – about as fast as your fingernails grow. Some mountain ranges, such as the Himalayas and the Alps, are still growing. Mount Everest grows by at least 1 cm every year.

▼ **The Matterhorn, in the Swiss Alps, has an unusual shape. The Alps formed when Italy and Europe pushed together. Glaciers then carved away the sides of the Matterhorn, leaving a pyramid shape.**

Wearing down

Mountains get worn down quicker than the land around them. High up on a mountain, the weather is very bad. Strong winds, rain and ice wear the rock and soil on a mountain's slopes away. A pointed peak on top of a mountain wears down until it is a smooth, rounded bump. The mountain's rocks and soil fall down valleys, and rivers wash them into the sea.

Wearing away mountains

Here are some of the things that wear down mountains.

- Wind blows soil and rocks away.
- Rain washes soil down slopes.
- Ice cracks rocks into smaller pieces which are blown or washed away.
- Animals wear down tracks and dig burrows.
- People wear away paths and scramble over rocks.

▲ This is Half Dome in California, USA. Its shape was probably made when glaciers scraped away half of the dome.

Location file

Krakatoa

In 1883, Krakatoa (below), an island volcano in Indonesia, exploded so violently that most of the mountain was destroyed. More than 36,000 people were killed on nearby islands, mostly by waves caused by the explosion.

Sudden changes

Sometimes a mountain wears down so much that a huge chunk of rock suddenly falls off. Volcanic mountains can also change shape suddenly. This happened to Mount St Helens, in the USA, in 1980. For many weeks magma built up inside the mountain, making it bulge on one side. Finally, on 18 May, the whole side of the mountain blew off. It was the biggest volcanic eruption in the history of the USA. Fifty-seven people were killed, and a lot of farmland and forest was destroyed.

◀ Small eruptions still take place at Krakatoa in Indonesia.

Volcanoes

Volcanoes form when magma from inside the Earth bursts out, or erupts. Every time a volcano erupts, it gets bigger and bigger.

Inside a volcano

Most volcanoes are cone-shaped, because rock and ash heap up around the spot where the magma comes out. When magma flows out of a volcano, it is known as lava.

Active, dormant or extinct ?

If a volcano is active, it means that people have seen it erupt. Stromboli in Italy and Arenal in Costa Rica are active volcanoes that erupt almost every day. A **dormant** volcano is one that hasn't erupted for a long time, but could erupt again. An **extinct** volcano is one that scientists think will never erupt again.

Where volcanoes form

Volcanoes often form near the edges of sections of the Earth's crust. Most of the world's active volcanoes are found in a ring around the Pacific Ocean. This ring is called the 'Ring of Fire'.

Volcanoes can also form where there is an area of extra-hot magma, called a 'hot spot', under the Earth's crust.

▼ This is what is left of Mount St Helens, in the USA. It exploded in 1980. You can see another mountain, Mount Rainier, in the distance.

Location file

Inner–city volcano

In Edinburgh in Scotland, UK, a castle stands on top of a giant rock in the middle of the city (above). The rock is actually the remains of a volcano.

Fact file

Famous volcanoes

Name	Place	Why is it famous?
Vesuvius	Italy	Erupted in AD 79, destroying the town of Pompeii.
Fuji	Japan	This beautiful volcano is considered sacred.
Mount St Helens	USA	Blew apart in an eruption in 1980.
Mauna Kea	Hawaii	Measured from the sea floor, this is the biggest volcano in the world.
Ojos del Salado	Chile	The world's highest volcano, measured from sea level.

Studying mountains

Studying mountains is not easy. You can't cut a mountain in half to see how it's made. But scientists have other ways of studying mountains.

Looking at shapes

Scientists can work out a lot about a mountain from the way it looks. If it's smooth and rounded, it's probably very old. Younger mountains are sharp and pointy.

Other shapes give clues about a mountain's past. For example, long, deep, U-shaped mountain valleys were made by glaciers – rivers of ice that move slowly down a mountain.

Layers of rock

A lot of the Earth's rock is made up of layers. Many of them were once layers of mud or sand. Over time they were squashed down into rock. Mountains push up these layers. Patterns in the layers show how rock has moved or folded. **Fossils** trapped in the layers can tell us when the rocks were formed.

These rocks in Yukon, Canada have many layers. Movements in the Earth have tilted and pushed them up.

Mountain scientists

Here are some of the different types of mountain scientists:

- **Geologists** study rocks and how they are made.
- **Geomorphologists** study the way the Earth changes.
- **Palaeontologists** study fossils, which can give clues about how old mountain rocks are.
- **Volcanologists** (right) study volcanoes and predict when they will erupt.

Volcano science

Volcanologists are scientists who try to predict eruptions. They check whether magma is building up inside a volcano. They study rocks taken from active volcanoes. Poisonous gases, flying rocks and lava can kill volcanologists. But they save many lives by warning people when a volcano is about to erupt.

People file

James Hutton

James Hutton (1726-1797) is often called 'the father of **geology**'. By studying rocks in Scotland where he lived, he realized that mountains were formed slowly by nature and changed over time.

Mapping mountains

map is a drawing of a place on a flat piece of paper. Mountains are hard to map for two reasons. Firstly, they are difficult to climb and measure. Secondly, mountains stick up from the ground, while a map is flat.

How high?

You don't need to climb a mountain to know how tall it is. The height of a mountain can be measured using triangles. If you know how far you are from a mountain, you can work out how tall it is. Today people use **lasers** to measure precisely. But different teams get different results, and people still disagree about how high a mountain really is.

Another way to measure a mountain is to look at the **air pressure**. This works because air pressure drops as you go higher up. The problem is that the weather affects air pressure, too.

▼ The diagram below shows how mountains are measured using triangles.

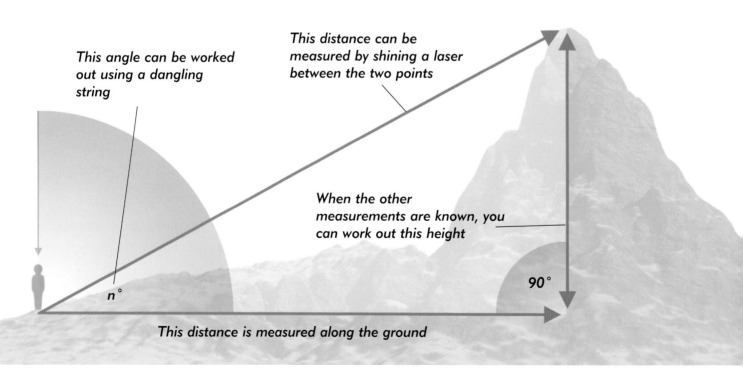

This angle can be worked out using a dangling string

This distance can be measured by shining a laser between the two points

When the other measurements are known, you can work out this height

$n°$

$90°$

This distance is measured along the ground

Mountains on maps

To show hills and mountains on a flat map, maps use special lines called contours. For example, a map can have a line for every 10 m of height. The closer the lines are together, the steeper the land is in real life.

Satellites and computers

Today many maps are made using **satellites**. Satellites in space can take photographs and measure the Earth. On the ground, GPS (Global Positioning System) gadgets help people to work out exactly where they are. This helps us to make better maps. Today we can also make **3D** maps on a computer.

▲ A mountaineer with his tent and sleeping bag halfway up K2, officially the world's second-highest mountain.

 Location file

Confusing K2

K2 in the Himalayas is the second-highest mountain in the world, but in 1987 it was measured at 8,851 m high – higher than Mount Everest. New measurements were taken in 1996. K2's official height is now 8,611 m.

Mountain zones

A big mountain can look different the higher it gets. Near the bottom a mountain is usually covered in forests. Higher up, there are meadows, rocky slopes, and finally snow and ice. These different levels are called zones.

Zones around the world

Mountain zones are different in different parts of the world. In hot countries, mountains usually have wet rain forests or dry grasslands near the bottom, then bamboo, flowers and **moorland** higher up. Mountains in cooler places – known as **temperate** – have forests lower down, then pine trees and meadows at the top.

The treeline

On high mountains, there is usually a line known as the treeline. Trees cannot grow above the treeline because it's too cold and windy for them. There is not much soil on the steep, rocky slopes high up, so there's nothing for tree roots to hold on to.

▼ This diagram shows the zones on a mountain. Hot, tropical zones are on the left and cooler zones are on the right.

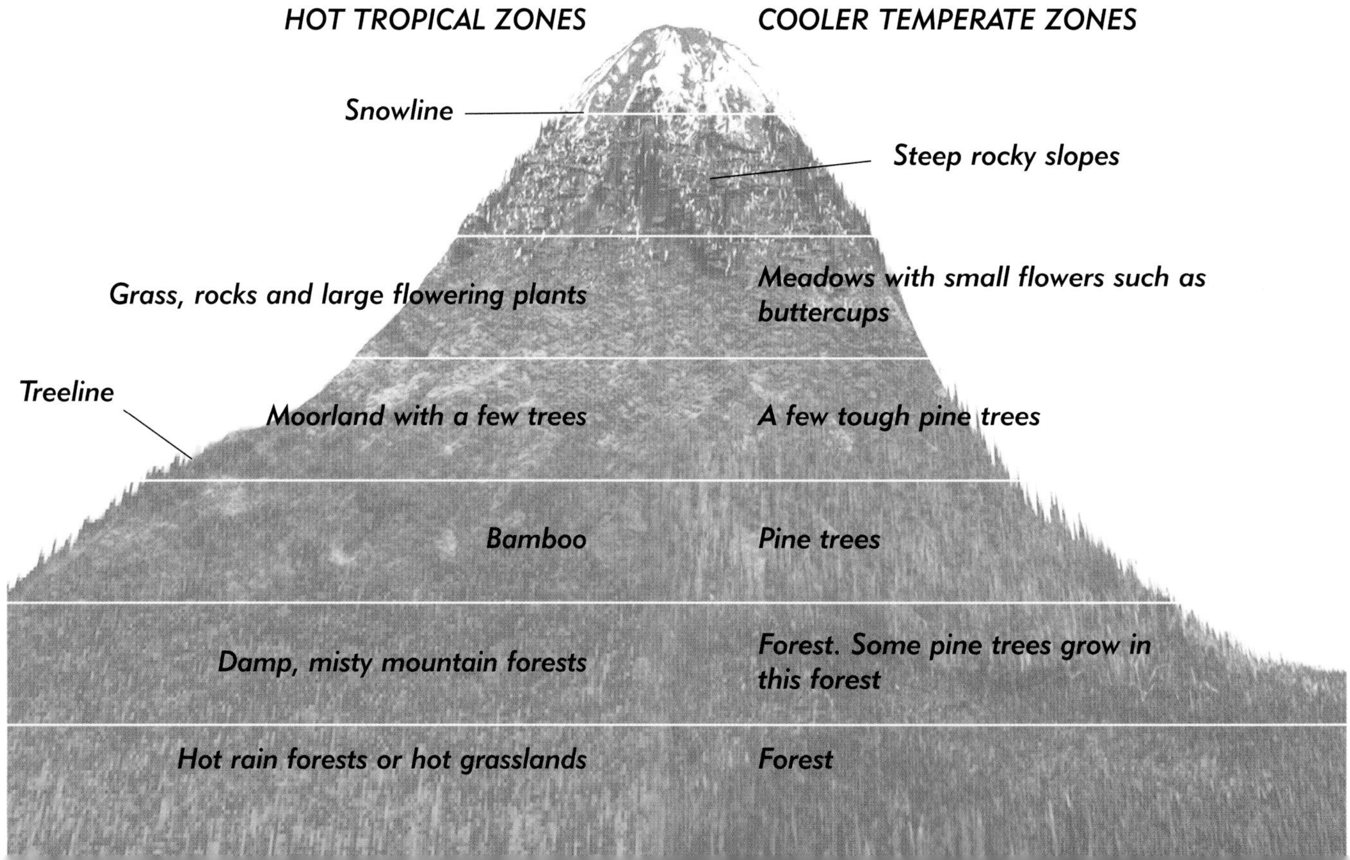

HOT TROPICAL ZONES   *COOLER TEMPERATE ZONES*

Snowline

Steep rocky slopes

Grass, rocks and large flowering plants

Meadows with small flowers such as buttercups

Treeline

Moorland with a few trees

A few tough pine trees

Bamboo

Pine trees

Damp, misty mountain forests

Forest. Some pine trees grow in this forest

Hot rain forests or hot grasslands

Forest

▲ In this photo, you can see three mountain zones. The meadow is at the bottom. Higher up you can see rocky slopes and snow at the top.

Snow and ice

Wherever they are in the world, the tops of high mountains are always covered with snow and ice. The area where snow and ice begin is called the snowline. Many mountains, such as the Alps, are completely covered in snow in winter.

Making rivers

Most big rivers form in the mountains. A river begins as a small mountain stream. As more streams flow into it, the stream gets bigger and becomes a river. When it reaches lower land, the river slows down until it ends up in the sea.

 Location file

Mount Egmont

Mount Egmont (left), also called Mount Taranaki, is a dormant volcano in New Zealand. It has many mountain zones.

◀ Mount Egmont, New Zealand.

Mountain wildlife

Mountains are home to many plants and animals. Different animals and plants are found at different levels.

Keeping warm

Mountains are cold so many mountain animals have extra-thick hair or fur. Yaks in the Himalayas have two layers of hair: a thick outer coat, and a soft, fluffy layer underneath. Snow leopards have fur even on the soles of their feet. Many animals can fluff up their fur or feathers to trap a layer of warm air around their bodies. Even some mountain plants have 'fur' to protect them from the cold.

Finding food

There is not much food on a mountain, especially in winter, so animals have to be good at finding it. Pikas – small animals similar to rabbits – collect grass in the summer, then dry it in the sun and store it to eat in winter. Lammergeiers (a type of vulture) feed on dead goats and sheep. Dall sheep can live on a winter diet of **lichen**, moss and frozen grass.

▶ These salmon are leaping up a waterfall in a mountain river.

Mountain animal facts

Here are some amazing mountain animals:

- Bar-headed geese fly over the tops of the Himalayas – as high as an airliner.
- Jumping spiders can live in the snow 7,000 m up on Mount Everest.
- Big rocks don't get in a cougar's way. It can jump 5 m straight up.
- Wild salmon can leap 3.5 m out of the water, up over waterfalls.
- A mountain iguana's body temperature can go down to 1.5 °C – almost freezing.

Plants on top

Mountain plants are usually stockier than other plants, with thicker stems and shorter branches. By clinging close to the ground they don't get damaged or blown away by the wind.

▲ Snow leopards live in high mountains in Asia, such as the Himalayas.

◄ A Japanese macaque, also known as a snow monkey, warms itself in a hot spring.

Location file

Monkey mountain

On the Shiga Kogen volcano, Japanese snow monkeys have found a great way to keep warm. They spend the day sitting in hot springs that bubble up between the volcanic rocks.

Living together

All the animals and plants that live in an area depend on each other to survive. This is also true on mountains. If an animal or plant disappears, it can affect other plants and animals in that area.

Food chains and webs

In the wild, animals eat either plants or other animals. Each living thing is food for another living thing. This is called the food chain. Plants are at the bottom of the chain and hunting animals are at the top.

Often more than one animal eats a kind of plant or another animal, so instead of a food chain it is called a **food web**.

Changing surroundings

Living things have to fit in with their surroundings. When the weather changes,

plants and animals have to change too. Brown bears, for example, eat different foods in different seasons. They eat eggs in spring, salmon in summer, and berries in the autumn. Some animals spend the cold mountain winters **hibernating** in a cosy den or burrow.

West Caucasian turs live in the Caucasus Mountains, in Eastern Europe. In summer, they live high up the mountain. In winter, they move lower down.

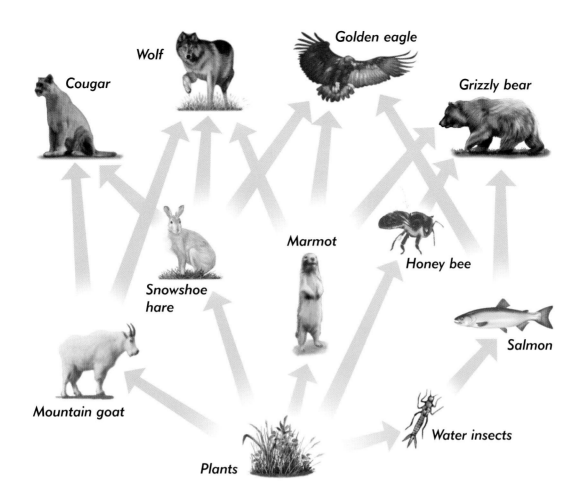

Wolf

Cougar

Golden eagle

Grizzly bear

Snowshoe hare

Marmot

Honey bee

Salmon

Mountain goat

Water insects

Plants

▲ This diagram shows a food web in a North American mountain forest. Each arrow points from something that is eaten to an animal that eats it.

Helping each other

Some living things help others to survive. Lichens, which cling to high mountain rocks, are actually made up of two living things, a fungus and an alga. The fungus, a type of mushroom, surrounds the alga, protecting it and keeping it damp. The alga, a type of tiny plant, uses sunlight to make food for both itself and the fungus.

Fact file

Food web levels
Living things are divided into different groups, depending on their place in the food web.

• **Consumers** Consumers is another word for 'eaters'.

• **Producers** Plants are called producers because they make (or produce) food using sunlight.

• **Decomposers** These include mushrooms and bacteria. They feed on dead plants and animals and help them to rot into the soil. This makes food for plants. Without decomposers, the world would be covered in dead animals and plants.

Mountain weather

Mountains have extreme weather: strong winds, freezing temperatures and snow. The shape of a mountain affects the weather.

The higher, the colder

It is much colder at the top of a mountain than at the bottom. Even at the **Equator**, very high mountains always have snow and ice on their peaks.

There are many reasons why it is colder high up on a mountain. The higher up you are, the thinner the air is. Thin air is cooler than air at ground level. Another reason is that the sun's rays hit mountain slopes at an angle, so they don't warm up much. The sun's rays bounce off rocky, icy mountain tops, too, so they don't heat up.

Rain catchers

As air moves close to a mountainside, it is forced upwards. As it rises, the air gets colder. The water in the air falls as rain or snow. So mountains are often very rainy. Sometimes, clouds cannot get past a mountain range. They drop all their rain on one side, and the other side becomes a desert.

▼ This drawing shows how a mountain range makes clouds, then rain or snow.

Air cools as it rises

Water in the air forms clouds. Water falls as rain.

Moist air blows in from sea

Ocean

Far side of the mountain doesn't get much rain and is called a rainshadow desert

Costa Rica cloudforest

In Costa Rica, the mountain forests, called cloudforests, are always covered in wet, misty clouds. The air is so damp that everything is covered with mosses and plants.

▶ **A cloudforest in Costa Rica.**

Why so windy?

On low land, trees, hills and buildings slow the wind down. High up, winds move much faster. By the time they hit a mountain, especially above the treeline, the winds are very strong. Winds speed up even more as they move around mountains.

Amazing weather

- The average temperature on top of Mount Everest is about –27 °C. At sea level in nearby Dhaka, the average temperature is 25 °C.
- Mount Washington in the USA is one of the world's windiest peaks. The wind there is around 70 kph, and can gust to 370 kph.
- The heaviest snowfall ever measured in a day – 190 cm – hit mountains in Colorado, USA in 1921.
- If a lot of snow falls on a mountain, it can form a glacier.

◀ **This glacier in Norway reaches the sea.**

Dangers and disasters

Mountains can be very dangerous. The steep slopes, cliffs, thick forests and bad weather make it easy to get lost or hurt. It's hard to get help if you do run into trouble. It is also dangerous to live at the bottom of a mountain.

Feeling the cold

Cold weather can be very dangerous for climbers. If it gets below about –5 °C, you can get frostbite. Frostbite can damage noses, fingers and toes so badly that they sometimes have to be cut off.

Dangerous drops

Mountains are full of places where it is easy to fall. As well as steep slopes, loose rocks and cliffs, high mountains have deep cracks in glaciers that can open up at any time. Climbers use special ladders to get across this ice.

Avalanche!

An avalanche is when a mass of snow slips off a mountain. Avalanches can kill skiers and climbers, and can cover whole villages.

▶ The British climber Alison Hargreaves, pictured on Mount Everest in 1995. She died later that year climbing another mountain, K2.

Location file

Deadly Everest

More than 150 climbers have died climbing Mount Everest. The worst disaster was on 10 May 1996, when a sudden storm blew over and eight climbers were killed.

▲ A mountain mudslide
in Boulder Creek, USA.

 Fact file

Mountain disasters

This table lists some of the worst mountain disasters in history.

Date	Place	Disaster
1883	Krakatoa, Indonesia	Volcanic eruption caused waves that killed 36,000 people.
1902	Mt Pelee, Martinique	30,000 people were buried under volcanic ash.
1985	Ruiz, Colombia	Eruption caused mudflows that killed 25,000 people.
1919	Kelut, Indonesia	Rock and mud from the volcano killed 5,000 people.
1963	Alps, Italy	Vaiont Dam overflowed when the hillside collapsed into it; 3,000 people died in floods.

▲ A mountain mudslide in Boulder Creek, USA.

Eruptions

When volcanoes suddenly erupt, they cause major disasters. As well as flinging out rock, ash and hot lava, volcanoes can cause massive mudflows. Mudflows happen when a thick layer of ash coats a steep slope and then gets rained on. The mud then slides down the mountain.

Using mountains

Mountains have precious rocks and useful plants and animals. They can provide energy too.

Precious rocks

Many useful rocks can be found in mountains. Because the rocks of a mountain have been pushed up, mountains are a great place to find precious stones and metals, such as gold, which are normally buried deep down. We also use other mountain rocks, such as granite, sandstone and limestone, for building.

Downhill power

Countries with lots of mountains can use them to make electricity. When water flows down mountains, it has a lot of energy. A **dam** can use the energy in a mountain river to make electricity. Over 90 per cent of Norway's energy is made this way.

A dam and power plant on the Kootenay River in the Rocky Mountains, Canada.

▲ Chinchillas come from the Andes mountains in Chile. Their fur is among the thickest and softest in the world.

Animal products

Because it is so thick and warm, hair or wool from mountain animals is often used to make luxury fabrics. For example, cashmere and pashmina wool come from Asian mountain goats. For a long time, people hunted other mountain animals, such as chinchillas and snow leopards, for their skins and fur. Many of these animals are now protected by law.

 Fact file

Mountain materials

Try and find these items in your house or area. They all come from mountains.

- **Pumice stone** Used for rubbing dead skin off your feet, pumice stone is made of lava.
- **Emeralds** Emeralds are green gems that are often found in mountain areas.
- **Aluminium foil** Made from bauxite, a **mineral** mined in the mountains of Jamaica and Brazil.
- **Marble** Used to make countertops and statues. It comes in many colours.

Mountain people

Mountains are tough places – but people do live there. They usually live in small villages that are difficult to reach. In the past, some mountain villages were so cut off that they had their own languages and customs.

Sheltered spots

Most mountain villages and homes are found in sheltered mountain valleys. Here they are protected from the worst of the wind, and are close to a river or stream. The highest villages in the world are in the Himalayas, about 5,500 m up.

Built for mountains

The higher up a mountain you go, the thinner the air is. But people who live in high mountains can cope with the thin air. They may even have bigger lungs than usual. People who live in the Andes have lungs up to 25 per cent bigger than ours. They also tend to be short and stocky, which helps them resist the cold.

Local porters carry luggage for mountain trekkers in Nepal.

Babu Chhiri

Babu Chhiri (far left) was a hero in his country, Nepal. He climbed Everest ten times in all, and in 2000 he set a world record for climbing Everest in the fastest time – just under 17 hours (it normally takes days). He died on Everest in 2001, aged 35, from a fall.

Earning a living

Many mountain people are farmers. They grow crops such as coffee, or raise tough animals, such as yaks, llamas or goats. Some mountain people work as guides and porters. This is especially true in the Himalayas, where the Sherpa people are famous for their climbing skills and knowledge of the mountains.

Fact file

Mountain nations

Here are some of the world's most mountainous countries:

- **Nepal** borders the highest Himalayan peaks.
- **Bolivia** around 60 percent of Bolivians live in the Andes mountains.
- **Ethiopia** has huge fault mountains on either side of Africa's Great Rift Valley.
- **Iran** has a ring of mountains around a central plain.
- **Switzerland**, in the Alps, is the most mountainous country in Europe.
- **Japan** is 90 per cent mountains.

▼ A market in an Andean mountain village.

Mountain towns

In the mountains, most people live in small towns or villages. Mountain houses are built to cope with wind, cold and heavy snow.

Mountain homes

Mountain houses usually have small windows and big roofs that stick out to stop snow from piling up against the door. In many mountain areas, homes are built on two storeys. The ground floor is used as a stable. The heat from the animals helps to warm the rooms upstairs. In the Alps, many houses have rocks stuck to their roofs to keep the snow from sliding off. Snow piled on the roof helps keep heat inside the house.

Mountain roads

Some slopes are very steep, so mountain roads slowly wind up them, twisting and turning. Travelling can take a long time. Where there's only a rough, steep track, animals are better than cars. Yaks, llamas or mules can carry heavy loads and passengers safely up and down the steepest mountains.

◀ Snow-covered wooden chalets (mountain cottages) in Switzerland.

Safe in the mountains

In the past, castles and walled towns were built on mountains to protect them from attacks. In Greece, for example, people lived by the sea, but they often built another town in the mountains where they could escape to in case of danger.

Machu Picchu

The ruined city of Machu Picchu, above, is 2,400 m up in the Andes in Peru, South America. It was built by the Inca people in the fifteenth century. It was deserted for more than 300 years, until it was rediscovered in 1911.

Mountain farms

Farming on a mountain is not easy. The soil gets blown away or washed down the slopes. Farm animals have to be tough. Still, there are millions of mountain farmers. Many of them grow just enough food for their families.

Mountain farm animals

Mountain farm animals are used to the tough conditions. In the Himalayas, farm yaks are related to wild yaks. Many farmers also keep mountain sheep and goats. In the Andes, farmers breed alpacas and llamas for their wool, milk and meat. Guinea pigs, which come from this area, are kept by some farmers for food.

Mountain crops

Mountain farmers grow crops that can cope with thin soil and cold, windy weather. The most popular crops include barley, quinoa (a type of cereal) and potatoes. A few crops, such as coffee and some types of berries, grow better the higher up they are.

◀ A mountain farmer in India harvests coffee beans.

Yak facts

The most useful mountain animal of all is probably the yak (right). It provides:

- Milk for drinking and making into butter. The butter is used as lamp fuel.
- Meat, eaten fresh or dried.
- Leather, used for making shoes and bags.
- Thick woolly hair, used to make rope, blankets and clothes.
- Dung, which can be used as fuel.
- Heat from its body warms the home.
- Transport.

▼ Mongolian farmers in Asia milk their yaks.

Terraces

Terraces are used on mountain farms around the world. These are small areas of level land, like steps, with walls to keep the soil from washing away.

◄ Bolivian farmers in the Andes harvest potatoes.

Up and down

In many mountain areas, farmers move their animals uphill in spring to feed on the fresh grass. In winter the animals are moved back down where it is warmer.

Mountain industries

T he precious stones, metals and wood in the mountains are useful. Mountain businesses range from big industries to small craftshops.

Mountain mining

Mining is a huge mountain industry. It can be very damaging. The hillside is bulldozed or blasted open to get to the precious stones and metals. At Cerro Rico (which means 'Rich Hill') in Bolivia, for example, so much silver has been mined that the mountain is 300 m shorter than it used to be.

Location file

The Muzo mine

The Andean town of Muzo, Colombia, is home to the world's biggest emerald mine. Thousands of local people make a living by picking through the leftover dirt for bits of emeralds.

▼ People search through rubble outside an emerald mine in Colombia, hoping to find emeralds.

Mountain crafts

In mountain areas, where it's hard to build factories, small crafts are very important. Common crafts are weaving and making clothes and leather goods. People use the hair and skin of sheep, yaks and goats. In the Atlas Mountains in North Africa, women weave rugs that can be sold to tourists.

Mountain wood

Trees are cut down for their wood all over the world. But as forests on lower land get used up, people are now cutting down mountain trees instead. This can cause problems on hillsides because the soil gets washed away easier if there are no trees to hold it back.

▲ Moroccan mountain weavers and rug-makers sell their wares in a city market.

People file

James Marshall

In 1848, carpenter James Marshall was building a sawmill on the American River in California, USA, when he found gold in the water. He tried to keep it a secret, but word got out and it started the California Gold Rush. Millions of people flocked to the Californian mountains hoping to find gold. Marshall never struck lucky again, and died poor.

Sports and tourism

Mountains attract millions of tourists every year. They are beautiful places to spend a holiday.

Amazing views

People like to climb mountains. There are wonderful views and amazing sights. In Hawaii, at Volcanoes National Park, tourists can see lava flowing from Kilauea, the world's most active volcano.

Exciting sports

Mountains are the perfect place for sports. The biggest mountain sport is skiing. Skiing resorts all over the world attract millions of tourists. Other sports include walking, climbing, snowboarding, white-water rafting and mountain biking.

Jobs in tourism

Tourism creates lots of jobs such as teaching people to ski and rock-climb, leading guided walks and working in hotels. There are more jobs in winter when there is lots of snow. In countries such as Canada, Switzerland, Nepal and Scotland, mountain tourism is very important.

▼ Tourists watch lava from a Hawaiian volcano flowing into the sea.

Extreme sports

Here are a few extreme and unusual mountain sports:

- **Canyoning** Wading, abseiling and swimming down a mountain river.
- **Zorbing** or **sphereing** Rolling down slopes inside a giant plastic ball.
- **Paragliding** Jumping off high places with a kind of parachute to float to the valley floor.
- **Ice climbing** Climbing up glaciers or frozen waterfalls.
- **Ziplining** Sliding through a valley while hanging from a cable.

▲▼ Snowboarding (above) and skiing are the most popular mountain sports.

Location file

Aspen, Colorado

In the 1930s Aspen, in the Rocky Mountains, USA, had a population of just 700 people. Then, in 1935, it began to be used for skiing. Today, it is one of the most famous skiing resorts in the world. The population of 7,000 increases to over 40,000 during the winter.

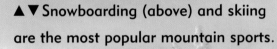

Caring for mountains

Mountain areas can easily be damaged by businesses, farming and tourism. Mountains areas have to be taken care of.

Ruining mountains

Many people enjoy going to the mountains on holiday. Tourism like this creates jobs for local people. But by building hotels, roads, ski-lifts and so on, people end up destroying the mountains they love. So we have to make sure that the changes we make do not ruin mountains or cause problems for wildlife.

National parks

A national park is an area that is protected from too much building. Many mountain regions are now national parks. National parks usually have toilets, litter bins and marked trails, so people can visit without causing damage or pollution. There are often park wardens who patrol the park.

Who owns mountains?

Mountain areas are often owned by the governments of the countries they are in. It is up to these governments to make laws to keep mountains safe and protect them.

Location file

Yellowstone

Yellowstone National Park, in the USA, is the oldest national park in the world. It was founded in 1872 and has nearly 3 million visitors a year. It is home to mountain animals such as wolves, bighorn sheep and grizzly bears.

▼ A park ranger at Yellowstone checks levels of air pollution in the park.

Unfortunately, many mountain areas are in countries where people are at war, such as in Afghanistan. It is hard for their governments to control mountain areas.

Location file

Scotland's Cairngorms

In the Cairngorm mountains in Scotland, some people wanted to build more skiing resorts and hotels to make money. Other people wanted to keep tourists out of some areas, because they could disturb rare mountain birds such as the golden eagle, snow bunting and capercaillie. In the end, the Cairngorms were made into a national park in 2003.

▲ A golden eagle, a rare mountain bird that lives in the Cairngorms.

Mountains in danger

Many mountain areas are being ruined by people and pollution.

Steep slopes

The trees and plants on a mountain's slopes stop soil from being washed away. But if all the trees are cut down, the soil can quickly wear away. This can harm whole mountain food webs, because animals need plants for their food. It can harm people too, because there isn't enough soil to grow crops. Sometimes loose rocks and soil crash down the mountain in a landslide.

Pollution from far away

Even mountains that are far away from cities can be harmed by pollution. The fumes from cars and factories rise up into the air and poison rainwater. Since it rains a lot in mountain areas, the poison from cities ends up there. It can damage forests and poison mountain lakes. Visitors to mountains can also cause pollution by leaving litter behind.

◀ Mountain forests in Washington State, USA, have been cut down, leaving bare hillside and destroying the home of mountain forest animals.

Messy Mount Everest

Since it was first climbed in 1953 by Sir Edmund Hillary and Tenzing Norgay, Mount Everest has become a dump. It is littered with plastic and rubbish. There are even dozens of dead bodies. Since 2000, many climbing expeditions have gone to Everest just to clean it up.

Wildlife in danger

Mountain plants and animals are well suited to living there. If their home is damaged – for example, if a mountain forest is chopped down for wood, or to make room for a ski slope – they have nowhere else to go and can die out. Some mountain animals are also illegally hunted for their fur, horns or meat.

Fact file

Rare mountain animals

Some mountain animals that could die out:

- Snow leopards in the Himalayas. They are hunted and their forests destroyed.
- Mountain gorillas in central Africa. They are hunted, and killed in wars and by disease.
- Giant pandas in China. The bamboo forests where they live are being cut down.
- Kakapos – flightless parrots that live in New Zealand – are killed by the cats and dogs people brought there.
- Grizzly bears in the USA. Killed in the past to protect people and farm animals.

◄ A rare wild giant panda.

Protecting mountains

Today, while some mountain areas are still in danger, governments and organizations around the world are trying to save them.

Parks and reserves

National parks help protect mountains by keeping them safe from hunting and overbuilding. Park rangers and wardens guard the parks and limit the number of tourists. Some countries also have special wildlife reserves, where rare animals are protected.

Conservation laws

Governments can also protect mountains with laws. For example, hunting rare wild animals such as snow leopards is now illegal in most countries. There are also laws that say people need permission to build a tourist resort. But it can be very difficult for governments to check that laws are obeyed in mountain areas.

In Sweden, every time a tree is cut down, another one is planted.

Rules for visitors

Many national parks have rules for their visitors. For example, if tourists stick to the paths, then other parts of the mountain aren't worn away by thousands of feet. Most parks also ask tourists not to start fires, leave litter or collect plants. At some times of year, certain areas of a national park may be closed so that animals can be left alone to raise their babies safely.

▶ A Nubian ibex with her calf.

Glossary

Abseiling A sport in which people climb down cliffs using a fixed rope.

Air pressure The weight of the air all around you. It is greatest at sea level and gets lower as you get higher.

Bacteria Very tiny living things.

Dam A wall built across a river or stream to hold back water.

Dormant Something that is sleeping.

Equator The place on Earth where the temperature is always hot. It is shown on a globe as a line all around the middle of the Earth.

Extinct If a type of plant or animal is extinct, it has died out forever.

Food web A way of showing how many animals eat other animals and plants.

Fossil The trace of a dead plant or animal visible in a rock that formed millions of years ago.

Geology The study of the Earth.

Glacier A river of ice that moves slowly down a mountain.

Hibernation A deep winter sleep. A hibernating animal doesn't move around, doesn't eat, breathes very slowly and has a lower body temperature than normal.

Laser A special ray of light.

Lichen A plant formed by a type of fungus and a type of alga living together. Lichens often look like light green/grey growths on the trunks of trees.

Magma Hot, molten rock inside the Earth. When magma surfaces, it is called lava.

Minerals Natural materials that form crystals. Sulphur, gold, silver, copper and diamond are all kinds of minerals.

Moorland An open area of boggy land with no trees.

Satellite A machine sent up into space to orbit the Earth. Some satellites are used to take photos of the Earth.

Temperate An area of the world that has cold winters and warm summers.

3D Three-dimensional.

Further information

Websites to visit

www.mountain.org/education/
The Learning About Mountains site is a fun guide to mountains, and has links to other sites where you can see videos of mountain animals and listen to mountain musical instruments.

www.nationalgeographic.com/ yellowstone/index.html
National Geographic magazine's children's site has lots of information about Yellowstone National Park, as well as activities and games.

www.fema.gov/kids/volcano.htm
Find out more about volcanoes and Mount St Helens on the children's website of the Federal Emergency Management Agency.

Books to read

Protecting Habitats: Mountains in Danger by Robert Snedden (Franklin Watts, 2005)

Earth's Changing Landscape: Earthquakes and Volcanoes by Chris Oxlade (Smart Apple Media, 2004)

Awesome Forces of Nature: Violent Volcanoes by Louise and Richard Spilsbury (Heinemann, 2004)

Mapping Earthforms: Mountains by Catherine Chambers and Nicholas Lapthorn (Heinemann, 2007)

Index